Remembering
Tucson

Mike Speelman

TURNER
PUBLISHING COMPANY

A view of the Santa Cruz Valley from the Carnegie Desert Botanical Laboratory on Tumamoc Hill.

Remembering
Tucson

Turner Publishing Company
www.turnerpublishing.com

Remembering Tucson

Copyright © 2010 Turner Publishing Company

Library of Congress Control Number: 2010924298

ISBN: 978-1-59652-645-7

Printed in the United States of America

ISBN 978-1-68336-896-0 (pbk.)

Contents

The San Xavier del Bac Mission complex, known as the White Dove of the Desert, and the vast Santa Cruz River Valley surrounding it, nine miles south of Tucson. Founded by Father Kino in 1692, the mission was built near a Tohono O'odham village.

Acknowledgments

This volume, *Remembering Tucson,* is the result of the cooperation and efforts of many individuals, organizations, and corporations. It is with great thanks that we acknowledge the valuable contributions of the following for their generous support:

Arizona Historical Society
Library of Congress

I wish to acknowledge the informed and patient assistance of the staff of the Research Library of the Arizona Historical Society in Tucson: Kate Reeve, Debbie Newman, Kim Frontz, Dave Tackenberg, Jill McCleary, and Chrystal Carpenter Burke, photo archivist supreme. I couldn't have done it without them.

PREFACE

Tucson has thousands of historic photographs that reside in archives, both locally and nationally. This book began with the observation that, while those photographs are of great interest to many, they are not easily accessible. During a time when Tucson is looking ahead and evaluating its future course, many people are asking, "How do we treat the past?" These decisions affect every aspect of the city—architecture, public spaces, commerce, infrastructure—and these, in turn, affect the way that people live their lives. This book seeks to provide easy access to a valuable, objective look into the history of Tucson.

The power of photographs is that they are less subjective than words in their treatment of history. Although the photographer can make subjective decisions regarding subject matter and how to capture and present it, photographs seldom interpret the past to the extent textual histories can. For this reason, photography is uniquely positioned to offer an original, untainted look at the past, allowing the viewer to learn for himself what the world was like a century or more ago.

This project represents countless hours of review and research. The researchers and writer have reviewed thousands of photographs in numerous archives. We greatly appreciate the generous assistance of the individuals and organizations listed in the acknowledgments of this work, without whom this project could not have been completed.

The goal in publishing this work is to provide broader access to this set of extraordinary photographs that seek to inspire, provide perspective, and evoke insight that might assist people who are responsible for determining Tucson's future. In addition, the book seeks to preserve the past with adequate respect and reverence.

With the exception of touching up imperfections that have accrued with the passage of time and cropping where necessary, no changes have been made. The focus and clarity of many images are limited to the technology and the ability of the photographer at the time they were recorded.

The work is divided into eras. Beginning with some of the earliest known photographs of Tucson, the first section records photographs through the end of the nineteenth century. The second section spans the beginning of the twentieth century through World War I. Section Three moves from the 1920s up to World War II in the 1940s.

In each of these sections we have made an effort to capture various aspects of life through our selection of photographs. People, commerce, transportation, infrastructure, religious institutions, and educational institutions have been included to provide a broad perspective.

We encourage readers to reflect as they go walking in Tucson, strolling through the city, its parks, and its neighborhoods. It is the publisher's hope that in utilizing this work, longtime residents will learn something new and that new residents will gain a perspective on where Tucson has been, so that each can contribute to its future.

—*Todd Bottorff, Publisher*

Ruins of the Quartermaster and Commissary buildings of Fort Lowell, ca. 1902. In March 1873, Camp Lowell, named for General Charles Russell Lowell, Jr., moved from Tucson east to the banks of the Rillito River. Designated a fort in April 1879, it was closed in 1892.

LIFE ON THE SOUTHWESTERN FRONTIER

(1870–1899)

Ruins of the Convento of the San Agustín de Tucson Mission. Also known as San Cosme de Tucson, it was built around 1800 and stood on the west bank of the Santa Cruz River near Sentinel Peak. Because of attacks by Apaches, this mission was abandoned by 1840.

The hospital at Fort Lowell was constructed during 1874 and 1875. It was an adobe building, with cool interior rooms and fifteen-foot ceilings. The wardroom held twelve to sixteen beds and there were smaller rooms for officers and special cases.

With its arrival in March 1880, the railroad changed the nature of travel and shipping in the southwestern desert. The arduous and expensive journey to reach Tucson was alleviated.

The *Arizona Citizen* began during a heated election campaign in October 1870 to oppose the *Weekly Arizonan,* Tucson's first newspaper. It became a daily in 1879, and is still published today as the *Tucson Citizen.* This office was located at 4 Plaza Square around 1880.

The San Xavier Hotel, built in 1881 for the convenience of train passengers, stood just north of the Southern Pacific Depot. The first hotel to have telephones and electric lights, it was a popular place for balls and receptions. The building was destroyed by fire in 1903.

The San Agustín Cathedral and Church Plaza around 1885. Designated a cathedral upon completion in 1868, the brick church had towers added in 1881 and a new facade in 1883. For many years, the Plaza was the site for the often rowdy Fiesta of San Agustín, Tucson's patron saint.

After failed attempts by others to build a railroad in Sonora, the Sonoran Railroad Company began operating in the early 1880s. Eventually running from Guaymas through Hermosillo to Nogales with a spur to Benson, the railroad provided service well into the twentieth century.

Looking west on Congress Street from Stone Avenue (ca. 1884).

Looking east along Congress (ca. 1885). The building with the extended roof is the Congress Street School, built in 1875. The Lexington Stable is in the distance. Tucson's large single male population created a pressing need for rooming establishments like the Congress Lodging House.

On November 8, 1887, Main Street was decorated for a parade honoring General Nelson A. Miles, commander of Arizona troops, for the surrender of Geronimo. Grateful citizens of Tucson and southern Arizona feted Miles with speeches and a ball, presenting him with a golden sword.

Mac Troy McCleary with Black Beauty, a trotting mare, in front of his home at 241 W. Franklin Street in 1888. In the early 1880s, McCleary was known as a gambler and ran the Shakespeare Club House. Eventually, he became a carpenter and contractor.

The San Xavier del Bac Mission (ca. 1890).

The San Agustín Cathedral and Church Plaza, perhaps just after a mass (ca. 1890).

The Southern Pacific Railroad Employees Reading Room on N. Third Avenue, just east of the SP Depot around 1890. Many railroad workers built houses in the vicinity.

Federico Ronstadt (center, in dark coat) organized the Club Filarmónico Tucsonense in 1889.
The Club began a series of weekly outdoor Sunday concerts in 1890 and made a two-week tour of
southern California to great acclaim in August 1896. The group disbanded in 1898.

As Tucson began to expand beyond the downtown area, architectural styles began to change, as seen in this neighborhood, looking to the northwest (ca. 1890).

Looking across the rooftops north of East Congress Street at North Stone Avenue (ca. 1893).

The front of San Xavier del Bac.

A view of the interior of San Xavier del Bac.

Looking across the rooftops to the southeast. The two-story building in the center background is a public school. The large open area is the Military Plaza where Camp Lowell was once located.

The Hose Company of the Tucson Volunteer Fire Department at a Fourth of July celebration in 1898.

Chemical Wagon #1 of the Tucson Volunteer Fire Department, July 4, 1898.

In October 1899, Andrew Carnegie gave Tucson a $25,000 grant to build a public library, as he did for many communities. The Carnegie Public Library building still stands today at 200 S. Sixth Avenue.

From Territory to Statehood

(1900–1919)

These north-facing businesses on Congress Street used canvas tarps both for advertising and to provide relief from the desert's harsh summer sun (ca. 1900).

Southern Pacific Railroad employees decorated a work shed for the Fourth of July.

A musical Fourth of July float paused in front of the Tucson Stables, owned by John Barkley (ca. 1900).

A Tucson Volunteer Fire Department hose and ladder wagon on Broadway Street (ca. 1904). Fire hydrants were installed on the streets beginning in 1883. The F. Ronstadt Co. was well-known throughout the Southwest for the quality of its wagons and carriages. At the far end of the building is E. J. Reese carriage- and sign-painting shop.

The Ramona Hotel at 34 S. Fifth Avenue, across from the Southern Pacific Depot, around 1905. The S. P. Barber Shop offered hot and cold baths to weary travelers.

Like many local businesses, the J. Knox Corbett Lumber Co. sponsored a baseball team (ca. 1905). Most games were played on the diamond at the Elysian Field, a south-side park formerly known as Carrillo's Garden.

The circular tuberculosis sanatorium at St. Mary's Hospital (ca. 1905). In 1880, the Sisters of St. Joseph built Arizona's first public hospital, west of Tucson, adding the sanatorium in 1900. The order came to Tucson in 1870, opening a school for girls and an orphanage.

A side view of the front steps of the St. Mary's Hospital Sanatorium (ca. 1918).

A crew smoothing concrete during the laying of tracks for the electric streetcar along Congress Street (ca. 1906).

A view of the Silver Bell Mine showing the Union Shaft, the power plant, and a test mill that could process ten tons a day (ca. 1908).

Built in 1907 after the original building burned down, the new Southern Pacific Depot on Toole Avenue is seen here not long after opening. Waiting for passengers along the street were both horse-drawn and motorized taxis.

Even Santa Claus had to make concessions to the desert in order to deliver his Christmas presents. A billboard touts a Dec. 14 appearance by the Lewis & Wolf Players. The Southern Pacific Depot is in the background (ca. 1907).

The southeast corner of Congress Street and Stone Avenue around 1908. Formerly the site of a saloon and a jewelry store, a new building was constructed in 1901 to house the Consolidated National Bank.

A group of African Americans posed in excursion automobiles before making a trip to San Xavier around 1909. San Xavier was a popular destination for picnickers and sightseers from Tucson and elsewhere.

The interior of the Cabinet Club at 68 W. Congress about 1910. The sign behind the bar advertised specialties of the house.

A tried-and-true method for crossing the Rillito after a flood took out the bridge on Oracle Road (ca. 1910).

Looking west on Congress Street from Scott Street, with a curio store on the corner (ca. 1910).

The ruins of the original San Agustín Mission continued to deteriorate. The Santa Cruz River flows in the foreground (ca. 1910).

The University of Arizona football team warming up before a game in 1910. Old Main, the University's first building in 1891, is in the background.

The paving crew at the El Paso and Southwestern Railroad Depot posed for a group picture in 1912.

Paving the concourse at the El Paso and Southwestern Railroad Depot, 1912.

The El Paso and Southwest Railroad Depot, Tucson's second station, around 1913. The adjoining, 2.6-acre Railroad Park was designed by Cammillo Fenzi Franceschi and contained many exotic plants and trees. In the background are Sentinel Peak on the left and Tumamoc Hill on the right.

The paving of Congress Street during 1913.

A view of Congress Street after the paving, looking west from Scott Street, around 1913. A trolley crosses Congress at Stone Avenue in the distance. There was still a mix of automobiles and horse-drawn vehicles in the streets.

Congress Street looking west from Sixth Avenue after paving (ca. 1914).

Freight and pickup trucks of local merchants on the concourse in front of the El Paso and Southwestern Depot around 1914.

A crowd gathers at the site of a one-car automobile accident on Mesilla Street around 1914. The Chicago Store was *una tienda barata* or a store with low prices. Across Meyer Street was the Lee Kwon & Co. grocery and dry goods store.

Built in 1913, the Hotel Tucsonia stood at Main Street and Congress Street near the El Paso and Southwestern Depot, seen here around 1915.

Around 1890, the Cosmopolitan Hotel was taken over by a Mrs. Orndorff who changed the name to the Hotel Orndorff. This view is around 1915.

Horse racing in its many forms has long been a favorite Tucson sporting event. Harness racing attracted a crowd at the new half-mile track at the Southern Arizona Fair Grounds (ca. 1915).

Eddie Rickenbacher was one of the competitors in a 103.152-mile auto race held March 20, 1915, at the Fair Grounds track. A few years later, he won the Medal of Honor as a World War I flying ace.

Congress Street looking east across Stone Avenue (ca. 1915). Automobiles quickly outnumbered horse-drawn wagons on Tucson's streets.

A float decorated for a convention of the Alianza Hispano Americana, a fraternal organization formed in Tucson in 1895. The banners and oars reflect its goals and standards. The girls wear sashes bearing the names of Arizona cities with chapters of the organization (ca 1916).

A float from a World War I parade.

The Tucson Police Department posed on the steps of City Hall with the first police motorcycle (ca. 1917).

A Liberty Bell float waiting for a World War I parade to begin.

Troops marching in a World War I parade. The El Paso and Southwestern Depot is in the background.

A night rally for Liberty Bonds on Congress Street around 1917.

A race car driver and his crew posed in front of the Schweitzer Machine Company on South Sixth
Avenue around 1917.

Looking west on Broadway Boulevard from Stone Avenue (ca. 1918). Broadway was still unpaved. The Broadway Rooms was formerly the Hotel Hall.

A multiracial float for a Fourth of July parade in 1918.

Between the Wars

(1920–1944)

As the summer desert heated up and humidity thickened, Mt. Lemmon in the Santa Catalina Mountains north of Tucson provided a cool retreat. Part of the Coronado National Forest, access by automobile became possible about 1920.

Formerly a mining claim and cattle ranch, the Flying V Ranch became a guest ranch in 1920, offering visitors a chance to experience the desert firsthand.

Stylish cowgirls got a taste of Southwestern life on a visit to the Flying V Guest Ranch.

The Tucson Citizen building at Stone Avenue and Jackson Street (ca. 1920).

The Alianza Hispano Americana float pausing during the 1920 Rodeo Parade.

The Hotel Arizona was constructed at 35 N. Sixth Avenue in 1917 and remained in business until 1986. Designed by Tucson architect Henry Jaastad, this is a view of the hotel around 1921.

Harold Bell Wright in front of his home.

Looking west on Congress Street from Stone Avenue around 1923. On the right, the Palace of Sweets offers homemade "Cactus Candy," a desert specialty.

A group of Rotarians from Prescott, Arizona, posed before San Xavier del Bac in the early 1920s.

Children pose in their flooded front yard as the Santa Cruz River overflowed its banks once again (ca.1925).

The University of Arizona swimming pool (ca. 1925).

By 1926, downtown traffic had become heavy enough at Congress Street and Sixth Avenue to require a traffic officer to direct vehicles. In May 1927, he would be replaced by the first traffic light.

Workers refurbishing the Southern Pacific Railroad tracks just west of the intersection of Sixth Street and Stone Avenue in the 1920s.

The Rodeo Parade making its way along Congress Street. The parade continues to the present day, though it no longer passes through the downtown area.

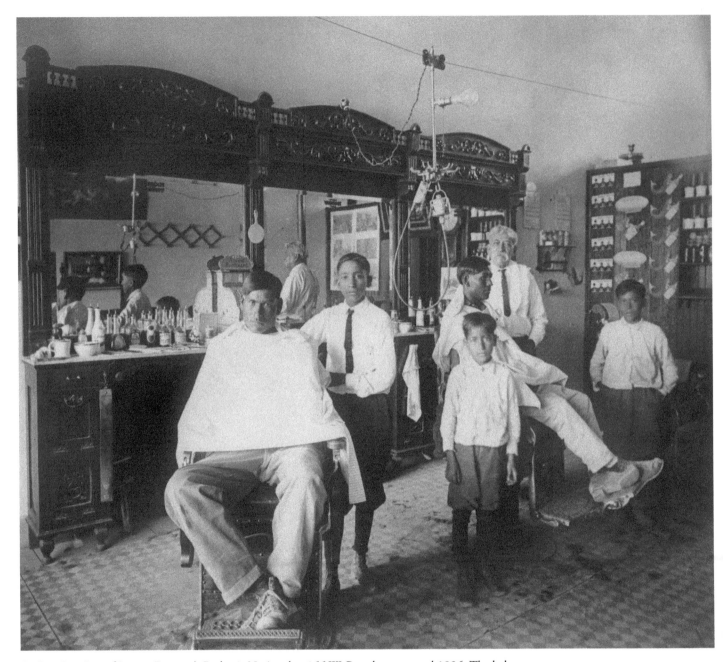

An interior view of Lazaro Romero's Barbaría Nacional at 166 W. Broadway around 1926. The helpers were Lazaro's sons.

A crowd greeted a special Christmas Train at the Southern Pacific Depot in December 1926.

The Southern Pacific Company Band preparing for a parade around 1927. This popular local band gave many outdoor concerts and was a staple in parades.

Looking south on Stone Avenue from Pennington Street around 1927. Electric trolleys, called "Izzers" because of their unique sound, ran on Tucson's streets from 1906 through the end of 1930.

Aviator Charles Lindbergh was honored with a parade in Tucson during his 1927 trip around the country following his record-setting crossing of the Atlantic Ocean.

Lindbergh's *Spirit of St. Louis* at the new Davis-Monthan Field in Tucson, September 23, 1927. He had come to help mark the opening of the airfield.

Standard Airlines made the first commercial flight to Tucson from Los Angeles, going by way of Phoenix, on November 28, 1927. Jack Frye, the president and chief pilot of the airline, is pictured with his wife.

A crowd gathered around a Fokker F-VIIb airplane at the Davis-Monthan Airfield in the late 1920s. This eight- to twelve-passenger aircraft was the most popular passenger plane of its time.

The front of the San Augustine Cathedral on South Stone Avenue, after two towers and a southwestern-style facade had been added to the original brick building in 1928.

When the luxurious, 150-room El Conquistador Hotel was built in 1928, it was still far outside the city limits. This is a picture taken not long after its opening.

Guests gather in front of El
Conquistador Hotel prior to a ride.

The Firestone Company airplane at the Tucson airfield around 1929.

Some motorized floats made an appearance in the early days of the Rodeo Parade, such as this Alianza Hispano Americana float in 1929.

A new building for the Consolidated National Bank was constructed on the site of the original at the southeast corner of Stone Avenue and Congress Street, beginning in February 1929. Tucson's first skyscraper, the building was eleven stories and still stands downtown.

Hollywood movies provided a needed distraction at the beginning of the Depression. In 1930, people line up to see *The Big Trail*, John Wayne's first starring role. The newly opened Fox Theater was Tucson's largest theater at the time.

New members gather in front of the Tucson Citizen building to mark the forming of a local chapter of the Mickey Mouse Club, sponsored by the *Citizen* and the Fox Theater, in July 1930. Walt Disney started Mickey Mouse clubs the previous year.

The Santa Rita Hotel and a view to the southeast (ca. 1930).

A man hung upside down to write on a blackboard posted over the entrance to the Arizona Daily Star offices at 33 W. Congress around 1930. The blackboard was used primarily for headlines and advertising.

Built in 1909 and remodeled in 1928, the Central Station of the Tucson Fire Department stood at 142 S. Sixth Avenue for many years.

Another view of the Central Station of the Tucson Fire Department.

The Bowen-Sime Motor Co. sold Studebakers and Pierce Arrows at the corner of Broadway Boulevard and Fifth Avenue (ca. 1930).

A view of Tucson looking northeast across the valley from Sentinel Peak (ca. 1930).

An art class taught by Edith Kitt uses San Xavier as a subject (ca. 1930). The church has long attracted the interest of artists and photographers.

A diamondback rattlesnake caught at Harold Bell Wright's camp at the foot of the Santa Catalina Mountains, near Ventana Canyon.

Looking north on Scott Street to Jacome's department store in the distance at Congress Street (ca. 1930). The wheel cover on the car by the lamppost in the foreground displays the Tucson Senior High School Badgers' football schedule.

As Tucson's population grew, so did the number of newspaper delivery boys needed by the *Citizen* (ca. 1930). Four motorcyclists took the papers to delivery points further away. Across the street was Louis May's Kosher Restaurant at Stone Avenue and Jackson Street.

At twelve stories with 220 rooms, Harold Steinfeld's Pioneer Hotel, at Stone Avenue and Pennington Street, became Tucson's second and tallest skyscraper of 1929. This view was taken around 1930. The Consolidated National Bank Building is in the background.

Karston the Magician headlines one of many Saturday afternoon stage shows, mixing live performances with movies, for Tucson children during the 1930s.

A view from the roof of the Consolidated National Bank at Congress and Stone streets, showing Tucson's expansion to the south in the early 1930s. The San Augustine Cathedral is in the foreground.

Archery was one of many sports the University of Arizona offered its students (ca. 1930).

As cars became faster, the Tucson Police used a squad of motorcycle police to help enforce the speed limit (ca. 1930). Tucson's first speed limit for automobiles, 7 mph, was set in 1903. The first speeding tickets were issued in 1920.

The Montgomery Ward & Co. building at Stone Avenue and Broadway Boulevard (ca. 1931).

Women who lost sons or husbands in World War I ride in the Armistice Day parade of 1932.

A touring Country and Western band from the Signal Oil Company radio show *Carefree Carnival*, during the early 1930s.

The Fox Theater decorated to promote the documentary feature *Bring 'Em Back Alive*, starring Frank Buck, in 1932. Ushers wore pith helmets and shorts.

Film comedian and character actor Roscoe Ates posed in N. Porter's Saddle and Harness Shop on Congress Street to promote his appearance in a movie in 1933.

Actress Jean Harlow posed before a stand of saguaro cactus while filming the movie *Bombshell* in Tucson in 1933. She was one of many Hollywood stars who found Tucson's climate and resorts inviting.

The participants in a men's bicycle contest gathered in front of the Fox Theater in 1933.

Women came into their own as pilots with the first Women's Air Derby in 1929. During the 1930s, air derbies became extremely popular around the country. Gladys O'Donnell, a well-known pilot, posed during a stop in Tucson.

120

The John Dillinger Gang made a court appearance after their capture on January 25, 1934.

A reluctant Harry Pierpoint, the member of Dillinger's gang who had suggested Tucson for a hideout, was forced to pose for photographers.

Though Dillinger himself had already been returned to Indiana by plane, a crowd gathered to watch the rest of his gang board the train to be extradited back to Ohio.

The third Pima County Courthouse built in 1929, seen here in 1934. The dome is made of glazed tile.

Frederick Maish and Thomas Driscoll built the Palace Hotel in 1875, luxurious by the standards of its day. Renamed the Occidental Hotel in 1894, this Tucson institution was torn down in 1935.

Tucson's usually mild winters made it a favorite on the horse racing circuit in the mid-1930s.

A group of boys uses the pool of the Arizona Inn for swimming and gymnastics (ca. 1938).

A scene from the movie *Arizona*. Many historical Tucson figures were portrayed in the film.

Dillon Ford, manager of the Hotel Congress, stands beside a Lincoln Zephyr (ca. 1940).

The Tucson Patriotic and Civic League hosted a watermelon party for 385 soldiers from Davis-Monthan Air Base on July 31, 1941. In addition, there were games and dancing on the women's athletic field at the University of Arizona.

Southern Pacific employees gathered to honor C. P. Kramer on his forty-fourth anniversary as an engineer with the railroad in April 1944.

NOTES ON THE PHOTOGRAPHS

These notes, listed by page number, attempt to include all aspects known of the photographs. Each of the photographs is identified by the page number, a title or description, photographer and collection, archive, and call or box number when applicable. Although every attempt was made to collect all data, in some cases complete data may have been unavailable due to the age and condition of some of the photographs and records.

II SANTA CRUZ VALLEY
Arizona Historical Society
B#32742

VI MISSION COMPLEX
Arizona Historical Society
B#201770

X FORT LOWELL
Arizona Historical Society
B#80337

2 MISSION RUINS
Arizona Historical Society
B#109477

3 FORT LOWELL HOSPITAL
Arizona Historical Society
B#93875

4 RAILROAD ENGINE
Arizona Historical Society
B#93528

5 ARIZONA CITIZEN
Arizona Historical Society
B#109358

6 SAN XAVIER HOTEL
Arizona Historical Society
B#207748

7 SAN AGUSTIN CATHEDRAL
Arizona Historical Society
B#111391

8 SONORAN RAILROAD
Arizona Historical Society
B#109331

9 CONGRESS STREET
Arizona Historical Society
B#200235

10 CONGRESS STREET SCHOOL
Arizona Historical Society
B#207749

11 MAIN STREET PARADE
Arizona Historical Society
B#207854

12 BLACK BEAUTY
Arizona Historical Society
B#44267

13 SAN XAVIER DEL BAC
Arizona Historical Society
B#111432

14 SAN AGUSTIN CATHEDRAL
Arizona Historical Society
B#27070

15 S&P READING ROOM
Arizona Historical Society
B#124

16 FEDERICO RONSTADT
Arizona Historical Society
B#111188

17 EXPANDING TUCSON
Arizona Historical Society
B#200223

18 EAST CONGRESS STREET
Arizona Historical Society
B#286a

19 SAN XAVIER DEL BAC
Arizona Historical Society
B#203225

20 CHURCH INTERIOR
Arizona Historical Society
B#201772

21 ROOFTOPS
Arizona Historical Society
B#109347

22 HOSE COMPANY
Arizona Historical Society
B#94485

23 CHEMICAL WAGON #1
Arizona Historical Society
B#94484

24 CARNEGIE PUBLIC LIBRARY
Arizona Historical Society
B#33336

25 CONGRESS STREET
Arizona Historical Society
B#91768

27 RAILROAD EMPLOYEES
Arizona Historical Society
B#109149

28 MUSIC FLOAT
Arizona Historical Society
B#109101

29 VOLUNTEER WAGON
Arizona Historical Society
B#205197

30 RAMONA HOTEL
Arizona Historical Society
B#38418

31 BASEBALL TEAM
Arizona Historical Society
B#94395

73 **Hotel Arizona**
Arizona Historical Society
B#39187

74 **Harold Bell Wright**
Arizona Historical Society
B#24901

75 **Congress Street**
Arizona Historical Society
B#39451

76 **Rotarians**
Arizona Historical Society
B#38726

77 **Flooded Front Yard**
Arizona Historical Society
B#33211

78 **Swimming Pool**
Arizona Historical Society
B#35887

79 **Congress Street**
Arizona Historical Society
B#27898

80 **Refurbishing Tracks**
Arizona Historical Society
B#203783

81 **Rodeo Parade**
Arizona Historical Society
B#110065

82 **Barbershop**
Arizona Historical Society
B#62396

83 **Christmas Train**
Arizona Historical Society
B#35566

84 **Southern Pacific Band**
Arizona Historical Society
B#32182

85 **Stone Avenue**
Arizona Historical Society
B#89556

86 **Charles Lindbergh**
Arizona Historical Society
B#93742b

87 **Spirit of St. Louis**
Arizona Historical Society
B#93724a

88 **Standard Airlines**
Arizona Historical Society
B#22105

89 **Fokker F-VIIb**
Arizona Historical Society
B#39027

90 **San Augustine Cathedral**
Arizona Historical Society
B#207711

91 **El Conquistador Hotel**
Arizona Historical Society
B#29010

92 **Gathering Guests**
Arizona Historical Society
B#203028

93 **Firestone Airplane**
Arizona Historical Society
B#35195

94 **Motorized Floats**
Arizona Historical Society
B#109977

95 **Consolidated National Bank**
Arizona Historical Society
B#7663

96 **"The Big Trail"**
Arizona Historical Society
B#35340

97 **Mickey Mouse Club**
Arizona Historical Society
B#35337

98 **Santa Rita Hotel**
Arizona Historical Society
B#24153

99 **Arizona Daily Star**
Arizona Historical Society
B#35113

100 **Central Station**
Arizona Historical Society
B#205198

101 **Central Station**
Arizona Historical Society
B#205193

102 **Bowen-Sime Motor Co.**
Arizona Historical Society
B#200586

103 **Tucson Valley**
Arizona Historical Society
B#200400

104 **Art Class**
Arizona Historical Society
B#203223

105 **Captured Rattlesnake**
Arizona Historical Society
B#38128

106 **Scott Street**
Arizona Historical Society
B#23505

107 **Citizen Paperboys**
Arizona Historical Society
B#33267

108 **Pioneer Hotel**
Arizona Historical Society
B#202953

109 KARSTON THE MAGICIAN
Arizona Historical Society
B#41488

110 STONE STREET
Arizona Historical Society
B#24701

111 ARCHERY CLASS
Arizona Historical Society
B#33429

112 POLICE MOTORCYCLES
Arizona Historical Society
B#29346a

113 MONTGOMERY WARD
Arizona Historical Society
B#200607

114 ARMISTICE DAY PARADE
Arizona Historical Society
B#204500

115 "CAREFREE CARNIVAL"
Arizona Historical Society
B#35414

116 FOX THEATER
Arizona Historical Society
B#24251

117 ROSCOE ATES
Arizona Historical Society
B#27413

118 JEAN HARLOW
Arizona Historical Society
B#34815

119 BICYCLE CONTEST
Arizona Historical Society
B#27340

120 WOMEN'S AIR DERBY
Arizona Historical Society
B#20775

121 DILLINGER GANG
Arizona Historical Society
B#28163

122 HARRY PIERPOINT
Arizona Historical Society
B#29104

123 DILLINGER GANG
Arizona Historical Society
B#28161

124 PIMA COUNTY COURTHOUSE
Arizona Historical Society
B#5274

125 PALACE HOTEL
Arizona Historical Society
B#200241

126 HORSE RACETRACK
Arizona Historical Society
B#40070

127 ARIZONA INN
Arizona Historical Society
B#27129

128 MOVIE SCENE
Arizona Historical Society
B#204565

129 DILLON FORD
Arizona Historical Society
B#25158

130 WATERMELON PARTY
Arizona Historical Society
B#9219

131 SOUTHERN PACIFIC
Arizona Historical Society
B#20687

Printed in the USA
CPSIA information can be obtained
at www.ICGtesting.com
JSHW072026140824
68134JS00042B/3798